White River Press
Amherst, Massachusetts

be clutter FREE

sorting made simple

by Rosalyn Cherry, M.S., C.H.T.

White River Press

Published by
White River Press LLC
PO Box 3561
Amherst, MA 01004
www.WhiteRiverPress.com

ISBN 978-1-935052-17-3

Printed in the US
Published September, 2009
Publication history:
First published by KathodeRay Media, Greenville, NY, 2009
Cover and Book Design by KathodeRay Media, Greenville, NY (www.kathoderay.com)

Dedicated to everyone who wants to live a simpler life.

When there is no clutter, you are surrounded by the things that nourish you. Everything has a place, so you can find what you need with ease. Your living space reflects who you are. You move forward in life, open to possibilities instead of being weighed down with too much. It is a glorious feeling of freedom and is attainable with time and effort.

THE WORLD'S BRIEFEST INTRODUCTION TO GETTING RID OF TOO MUCH STUFF

You have in your hand a color-coded step-by-step **ACTION PLAN** to *be clutter FREE*. The only way to have less stuff is to take action to let go of the stuff you have.

Go to **QUICK START** on page 1 and Jump In
or go to **GET SET! PACE** on page 9 and Ease On Down the Road.

They both take you to the same place - building your de-clutter muscle to let go of your stuff.

And there is support on

page 7 with a **SAMPLE SESSION**.

page 12 with **HELP FOR THE OVERWHELMED**.

page 21 with **THE STAY ENGAGED STAGE** to prevent emotional and technical blocks. What are you saying to yourself?

page 24 with **TIPS FOR DE-CLUTTERING**, a comprehensive list of strategies to become and stay motivated to take action.

page 33 with **NEW STUFF?** to practice immediately to not build up any more new clutter, even if you aren't clutter free yet.

page 37 with client **EXPERIENCES** of how others like you followed the *be clutter FREE* action steps.

TABLE OF CONTENTS

TABLE OF CONTENTS

QUICK START

Jump In

To be clutter free is to discover what works for you and what makes your life manageable. My advice is firmly grounded in the real world by offering easy-to-follow action steps, client experiences and motivational strategies to match your personality and current habits, goals and needs.

Take a moment to look around you. Do you notice anything that seems cluttered or out of order and that you would like to change? If so, let's take 15 minutes to de-clutter a shelf, a countertop or a chair piled with unrelated items right now! Read below and turn the page to start.

Five guidelines to remember:

1. **Keep only what is useful**, adds to your life and reflects who you are.

2. **Take small** manageable steps.

3. **Only do as much** as the time you have allocated allows.

4. **Take consistent action** over time.

5. **Follow through giving yourself rewards**. Rewards are an integral part of both changing and sustaining new habits.

Tip:

The only way to learn how to cook and bake is to follow a recipe. The same is true with letting go of clutter. By following the *be clutter FREE* action steps in this guide you will begin to learn how to build your de-clutter muscle and live clutter free.

Create Your Sorting Cards

Cut out the cards on the following page or copy the categories on index cards or post-its. They represent the possible categories for items you will be sorting. They are used during **The Decide Ride** where you sort items into piles and again in **The Wrap-Up Wrap** when the grouped piles are distributed.

You will be creating cards with the following labels:

Trash	**Give Away**
Sell	**Treasure Chest**
Keep Here	**Repair**
Keep Elsewhere	**Special Hold Box**

Trash

Give Away

Sell

Treasure Chest

Keep Here

Repair

Keep Elsewhere

Special Hold Box

QUICK START

be clutter FREE Cheat Sheet

Do you want to get started right away? Contained below are all of the "basics" of the *be clutter FREE* method. If you want to go slower, turn to **Get Set! Pace** on page 9.

Choose a "clutter knot" that you know you can successfully de-clutter within the next 15 minutes. This is often one shelf, one drawer, one corner of a table or a small pile of unrelated items. This is called your Target Area.

Remove all the items from the Target Area so the area is completely cleared. *Don't jump up and put these items away – yet!* Clean your Target Area with a quick wipe or dusting.

Decide what goes or stays. Lay your Sorting Cards from page 2 around you, or attach them to boxes or strong standing paper bags. Then one item at a time, decide what to let go or to keep and place the item next to the appropriate Sorting Card. Not sure what a sorting card is? Not sure how to decide? Turn to **The Decide Ride** on page 15.

Let Go Items:	Trash, Give Away, Sell
Keep Items:	Keep Here, Keep Elsewhere, Treasure Chest, Repair
Special Hold Box:	For items you are not sure if you should let go or keep.

QUICK START

Getting Stuck or Overwhelmed? Read **Help for the Overwhelmed** on pages 12 and 13. Still stuck? See the **Sample Session** on the next page. Also **The Stay Engaged Stage** chapter on page 21 to help you keep going.

Piles away.

The items to Keep Here in the Target Area can all be returned.

Grab the items to Keep Elsewhere in your home. Walk around quickly and place items in or near where they belong. Do NOT organize the new area.

Put Give Away and Sell items in boxes or bags you can't see through and seal them. Determine how will you arrange for these items to leave your home.

Take out the Trash. Tie it up and immediately put it out with the garbage.

Not sure what to do? Turn to **The Decide Ride** on pages 17 and 18.

Schedule your next session. Energized? Motivated? Have more time?

Choose your next "clutter knot" and begin another session right now.

Reward! Make sure to reward yourself. Don't buy a new CD or DVD, instead go

to a movie or museum, meet a friend or watch a sunset!

QUICK START

Sample 30 Minute Session

Target Area: Top shelf of bookcase

Prepare your Target Area. Clean and clear area, put all items on a nearby table. Get a chair, grab a trash bag and lay out Sorting Cards.

What will stay in this Target Area?
Travel books, maps and framed travel photos

Choose what items go or stay and place in the appropriate pile, until you have no more items.

Piles Away! Distribute Items
Keep Here – Photos and current or favorite travel books and maps

Keep Elsewhere – Photos to office

Keep Elsewhere – Photos to country house

Repair – Special family antique frame

Trash – Outdated books and brochures, faded or torn photos and old broken frames

Sell – New timely travel books never used

Give Away – National Geographic to schools

Give Away – Give photos to sister

Give Away – Snow globe collection to children's hospital wing

Treasure Chest – Journal from Cuban trip

Schedule next session for tomorrow after dinner.

Reward by having brunch with best friend.

GET SET! PACE

Your Time Block

How long? Be reasonable and realistic – you know how much time you can spare, and you know your limits.

Start with small Time Blocks, such as 15 minutes, to learn the method. Over time as you start to see results it will be easy to increase your Time Blocks.

When? Be honest with yourself. What part of the day are you more alert? You can experiment with 15 minute blocks at different times.

Take consistent action over time. By spending as little as 15 minutes of your time, every morning or evening, at least every other day, you will be inspired as you learn the method and watch your clutter disappear.

Pace yourself. Be fair to yourself and use sensible Time Blocks you know you can stick with. Keep following the method and build momentum week after week.

GET SET! PACE

Tip:

Start small. You don't have to tackle the whole job at once. Break it up into small, manageable sessions.

Choose Your Target Area

Match your Target Area to your time. Set yourself up for success – don't take out more clutter than you can go through in your Time Block.

For Example:
- Instead of the whole desk, start with a drawer
- Instead of the whole kitchen, start with a kitchen counter
- Instead of the whole closet floor, start with a corner

GET SET! PACE

Prepare Your Target Area

Remove all the items from the Target Area so the area is completely cleared. Don't jump up and put these items away – yet! Clean your Target Area with a quick wipe or dusting.

Get comfortable. How about some upbeat energizing music? Place a chair or stool right next to your Target Area. Or you can sit on the floor.

Open your trash bag and set out the Sorting Cards from page 2 within reach. You can put these cards on the floor, or attach them to boxes or strong standing paper shopping bags.

If moving along, skip ahead to the **Decide Ride** on page 15.

If you're unsure or stuck, continue to **Help for the Overwhelmed** on the following pages.

GET SET! PACE

Help for the Overwhelmed

Getting started can often be the hardest part of the de-cluttering process. To assist, we have included client Experiences that show what others did to begin becoming clutter free.

Go to page 37 and read one or more of the stories. Notice the strategies used. Notice how these clients chose specific *be clutter FREE* action steps to move themselves forward into the de-cluttering process. Notice Brian, Dara and Maria were not prepared to jump right in. Using the *be clutter FREE* method they overcame their blocks with a realistic plan and a sensible pace.

Brian looked at Tips for De-cluttering and realized he needed to make a detailed plan and find a buddy for accountability. Jen found a buddy to keep her focused. June was inspired by following the Sample Session and started sorting. Both Susan and Dara went to QuickStart with unmanageable "clutter knots" and built on these first successes. Maria chose to make the best of her situation using *be clutter FREE*.

Remember:

Don't get discouraged, take small steps. 15 minutes here and 15 minutes there can really add up. Every step helps you build a stronger de-clutter muscle.

GET SET! PACE

More Help for the Overwhelmed

Are you experiencing strong emotions? Go to **The Stay Engaged Stage** and look at the Emotional Blocks on page 22 and 23. Do any of these apply to you? Are they familiar? Does telling yourself something different help?

Think about the **Tips for De-cluttering**. What about making a list of how your life will change when you are de-cluttered? Or making a Vision Board to help you visualize the goals of what you want to create in your life?

Look over the list of strategies for becoming and staying motivated. Begin with one, any one on pages 25 to 27. The key to becoming clutter free is to stay engaged in the process of de-cluttering even if you are having a rocky start or shaky session.

And how do we get there?

If you have your Time Block and Target Area chosen and ready go to **The Decide Ride** on page 15.

THE DECIDE RIDE

To Let Go or To Keep?

Review each item in Your Target Area and go through this decision-making process: to let go or to keep? Then place the item in the correct Pile.

We encourage you to let go. Most clutter is just not useful – or it wouldn't be sitting in your Target Area.

Let Go or Keep? If an item is no longer useful, no longer adds to your life, or no longer reflects who you are, then put it in your Let Go Pile.

Tip:

Begin with one item at a time in your Target Area. If you try to focus on a group of items, you may find difficulty letting go, but by looking at each item independently, you might find there are more items in your Let Go Pile.

Meet Your Piles

Let Go Pile

When you let go of items thank them for their contribution to your life and wave good-bye. Items that you toss or let go of fit into three categories:

Trash.   Give it away.   Sell it.

Any opportunity this book presents to let go—think green first. Make a decision that is best for the environment.

When planning to sell an item, think of this: is it worth your time and energy selling items on eBay or Craigslist? Will you have the time and energy to plan a yard sale? It might be easier to give an item away instead.

Are you having trouble letting go of your stuff? Often if you choose where an item will go (to a hospital or to survivors of a natural disaster) it is much easier to let go. And reusing is good for the environment.

Would taking photographs of the item help to let go? In Experiences read about Dara who used photographs to clear out a large trunk of possessions to which she was deeply and emotionally attached.

Tip:

If you have unfinished projects say to yourself, "Will I really finish this? Why haven't I done it already?" Set realistic completion dates or let them go. Donate to a children's center or nursing home. It's better to pass them on.

THE DECIDE RIDE

Keeper Pile

The Keepers fall into these categories:

Keep Here. Items will stay in this Target Area. They can be returned one by one as each item is examined, or they can be returned as a group after all items in the Target Area are examined.

Keep Elsewhere. Items to be kept in another room, another site (office, school, car or second home).

Treasure Chest. This is a box or drawer for sentimental items. You may find as you accumulate more and more mementos you can prioritize and let go of the less nostalgic items.

Repair. Items once they are mended, sewn, repaired, washed or dry cleaned can be returned to where they belong. However, be realistic and reasonable. Will you really fix this? If you think so, why haven't you done it already?

You may determine that items in your Keeper Pile need to be placed in a storage rental facility. Wait until you have gone through everything before evaluating if you need storage. As you build your de-clutter muscle think about the possibility of not storing by putting these items in your Let Go Pile. Remember there are others who can use these items now. Otherwise consider all the pros and cons before deciding to use a storage rental facility.

Special Hold Box

If you cannot decide to let go or to keep items you can designate a Special Hold Box.

Put this box with the undecided items listed on the front away with a date for when you will check it in four to eight months. Put this date on your calendar. If you do not miss these items by the appointed date then let them go.

You could also include items

to which you are emotionally attached. Experiment with the idea that these items are no longer useful in your life. Having these items intentionally placed here "on hold" could help you get a perspective on letting them go. When you go back you may be surprised that you are more easily able to let go.

Be gentle and non-judgmental.

It is understandable that you feel stuck or frustrated deciding about certain items. Keep moving forward. You do not have to be perfect. You are developing your ability to distinguish what is useful, truly adds to your life and reflects who you are.

THE DECIDE RIDE

Think Again?

You always have the option to change your mind and toss out items you thought you wanted to keep. Sometimes when you ask yourself a second time (think again?) you can let go. Try to get rid of as much as you can when in **The Decide Ride** cycle.

As you continue to build your de-clutter muscle, letting go will naturally become a habit with time and practice. This behavior of letting go becomes second nature, so every time you think again and let go you are reinforcing this new habit.

There is a whole body of research on changing habits, which is sometimes referred to as changing the neural pathways. It is something you might like to explore on your own to help deepen your understanding of what you are doing as you continue to let go.

If there are no more items to examine then go to **The Wrap-Up Wrap** on page 29.

If there are more items, you will stay in **The Decide Ride** cycle, using **The Stay Engaged Stage** chapter for tips and inspiration when needed.

What is The Stay Engaged Stage?

This is a treasure trove of encouragement and motivation. Take a look – even if you are speeding along – it always helps to add a little extra muscle to your **Decide Ride**, pages 15 to 19.

Come here for support and reinforcement to stay engaged any time during the de-cluttering process, especially if you get stuck in the following ways:

Emotional Blocks. What you think, feel or believe to be true. For emotional attachment explore what you are saying to yourself about the de-cluttering process itself on page 22 and about a specific item on page 23.

Technical Blocks. Losing track of the de-cluttering process or getting confused about your next step? Turn to page 24.

Emotional Blocks

What are you saying to yourself about the de-cluttering process itself?

"This is not a good time for me. I don't feel like doing this right now. Maybe over the summer."

Instead try: "I'll start with baby steps and who knows how far I will get by the summer."

"There's something else I need to do right now."

Instead try: "I will spend the next fifteen minutes going through my stuff. Then I can do my errand."

"This is really hard for me to do. I get so overwhelmed. I feel so stupid"

Instead try: "Now I have the tools and I do not need to feel stuck. The **Quick Start** section on page 1 is a good place to start. I can jump right in and see what happens."

"There's just too much here. It feels hopeless. How will I ever get out of all this mess?"

Instead try: "I don't have to think about that. I only need to think about what I can do today. I can begin with one item and try a few more after that."

Tip:

When June in **Experiences** found she had so many items she did not like or use, her usual pattern was to get mad at herself and stop in her tracks. She took advantage of the built-in support in **The Stay Engaged Stage** to keep out of her old familiar trap.

THE STAY ENGAGED STAGE be clutter FREE

What are you saying to yourself about a specific item?

Helpful replies to use when you are stuck. Remember if you are not sure what to do with an item do not let that discourage you. You will always have another chance to decide to discard it, keep it or put it in the Special Hold Box. Move on to the next item in your Target Area.

Will this matter in five years?
I can let it go.

I haven't used this in a year.
I can let it go.

It may be sentimental but I cannot keep everything in my Treasure Chest.
I can prioritize and let go of the less significant.

If I need it one day I can borrow it or easily get a new one.
I can let it go.

How many more times am I going to have to think about this?
I can let it go.

Leading a simpler life is priceless.
I can let it go.

Here are some suggestions for the hardest items to let go of such as gifts, clothes and books. If you are prepared with places where these items will be taken it often makes it easier to let go.

Gifts: These are the gifts that you do not use, like or add to your life. It can help to put these gifts in their own Special Hold Box, page 18. You'll then get used to the idea of letting them go to a place where they will be valued and treasured.

Clothes: If you knew how and where your clothes would be recycled it often makes letting go easier. Research where there are thrift and consignment shops, what are their hours and how will you get items there? Can you arrange a pick-up?

Books: Find in your community all the facilities where books are accepted. And how will you get the books to each facility? You may want to sell books on Craigslist or Amazon. Be sure you have the time to do this so these books do not sit around and become clutter.

www.BeClutterFreeBook.com • 23

Technical Blocks

Are you losing track of the method or getting confused about your next step? The color-coded Table of Contents breaks the process into smaller steps. Here's a quick summary:

Get Set! Pace pages 9-13

Choose a Time Block and a Target Area.
Remove all the items and quickly clean area.

The Decide Ride pages 15-19

Decide what goes or stays.

Let Go items:	Trash, Give Away, Sell
Keep Items:	Keep Here, Keep Elsewhere, Treasure Chest, Repair
Special Hold Box:	For items you are not sure if you should let go or keep.

The Wrap-Up Wrap pages 29-31

Distribute piles and take out trash.
Set up next session and reward.

The strategies on the next page can be helpful in providing insight, inspiration or a fresh new outlook.

Tips for De-cluttering

Wherever you are in the de-cluttering process, whether you still feel unsure or you're feeling confident, you can use the strategies below for becoming and staying motivated. Adapt them as you build up your experiences with de-cluttering. What inspires you and keeps you engaged in the de-cluttering process may change and evolve over time so check back often.

This is your process and as you learn more about yourself you will be able to develop approaches that create successes and eliminate what doesn't work or move you forward. Your ability to identify what is important to you will add to your life and free you up for new experiences.

Get a buddy for accountability or find a buddy who also wants to de-clutter. Find someone to whom you can report your progress and from whom you can get some direction. Or you can make plans to hold each other accountable and even work side-by-side helping and supporting each other in your de-cluttering project.

Write down your motivations for de-cluttering. Post this list where you can see it. Modify as needed.

THE STAY ENGAGED STAGE

Stop thinking and do something. Keep yourself engaged. Take some action and observe what happens. Surprise yourself with your creativity.

Keep a log to track your successes and motivate your next steps. This log of completed sessions/tasks can include how much time was spent, if were you motivated by your reward and anything else helpful you observe.

List the ways your life will change when you are de-cluttered. Review this list as you progress. Keep it updated as you open up to new experiences.

Buy a label maker and make fun and colorful labels.

Can't let go? **Take a picture and wave good-bye.**

Design a long term plan with every major task broken down into its smallest steps. If it would also be helpful set target dates for completion. It's OK if something takes longer than anticipated. Adjust the date and don't beat yourself up.

Create a Vision Board. Make a scapbook or on a large poster board put inspiring photos, sketches and phrases that help you visualize the goals of what you want to create in your life.

THE STAY ENGAGED STAGE

Put together a fun basket you take out whenever you are de-cluttering. It could include a CD of upbeat energizing music, a tape measure, a timer, a label maker, scissors, a marker and cardboard to make signs and reminders or whatever else might motivate you.

Keep a "never thought I could let it go" list. Create a running list of the items that were difficult to let go, what they represented to you and what you did with them. Keep it updated and post it for inspiration.

Get rid of distractions like the cell phone or an engrossing movie on TV.

Add your own ways to be successful and Stay Engaged:

Way to go! Your session is almost completed.

Distribute Piles (Piles Away)

All items that are to Remain Here in this Target Area can all be placed in their final location.

Grab the items to be Kept Elsewhere **in your home**. Walk around quickly and place items in or near where they belong.

Avoid zigzag organizing. If you come across an item that belongs elsewhere and is not part of the Target Area you are completing, don't stop to de-clutter it. Jen in **Experiences** represents a perfect example of the perils of zigzagging.

Grab the items to be Kept Elsewhere **outside your home**. Quickly place them in a sturdy bag or box and put them with your briefcase (if they belong at the office) or with your car keys (if they belong in the car). Put other items near the door to ensure their movement out of your space.

Get the Repair pile. If items need to be washed pile them in with the next load. Place items to be dry cleaned or otherwise sent out for repair neatly near the door. Be sure to get these items taken care of so they do not become clutter.

Give Away and Sell. Put all these items in boxes or bags you can't see through. Label and seal them. Can you arrange for these items to be picked up? Otherwise how will they leave your home? For items to be sold, set a date by which you will do this. If these items are allowed to sit around waiting to go to their next home they can become clutter.

Finally the Trash! Tie it up and immediately put it out with the garbage. Avoid second thoughts by using opaque trash bags where you can't see through the bag and have the chance to rethink what you have already tossed. Be sure to have more trash bags for your next de-cluttering session.

Your Next Session

Doesn't it feel great to be de-cluttering? Build on the good feelings and the momentum you've created – decide on your next Time Block and Target Area. Make an appointment with yourself now – mark it on your calendar.

Energized? Motivated? Excited? Have more time? Go to Get Set! Pace and begin another session right now. Reward! Continue on next page.

THE WRAP-UP WRAP

You Deserve a Reward

Give yourself the reinforcement and support needed to change habits over time – reward yourself. Decide how you will treat yourself when your session is completed.

You may want to make and post a large colorful sign to remind yourself about rewards. Or post a chart of tasks and rewards.

Make this fun. Be creative and inspire yourself. You know best how to motivate yourself. Be outrageous. Whatever it takes, keep yourself engaged in the de-cluttering process.

Avoid rewarding yourself with items that can become clutter – do you really need another CD or DVD? More make-up? Another pair of shoes? Instead, break the clutter habit! Get a manicure, go to a movie or museum, rent a bike, meet a friend for a cup of coffee, take a walk or shoot some hoops.

New Stuff?

To continue to **be clutter FREE**, before you bring a new item into your living space, regardless if it is a purchase or an unsolicited gift, **stop and decide**. Start this practice immediately so you do not build up any more new clutter, even if you aren't clutter free yet.

Stop and decide

Let Go? Keep? How will this item add to your life? Would it be useful? Does it reflect who you are? Do you have a place for it?

Are you sure you want it? If not, good for you! Nothing to buy or bring in.

Let go of an another item whenever you bring a new item in. Thank the item that is being let go of for what it has brought to your life. Maybe you can let go of two items for each new item you bring into your life. Three? or More?

Find a place for this new item. Always return the item to its designated place.

Enjoy!

Stuff Out of Control?

If your stuff continues to get re-cluttered, you can begin again with immediate action by going to **Get Set! Pace** on page 9. You can think about what worked and what did not work. What did you do that was successful? The key is to keep taking positive action and not become discouraged.

There are no universal rules for de-cluttering. Everybody's living situation is different and what works for one person might not work for another. As skills, habits, goals and needs change priorities may shift. It is important that you keep yourself immersed in the process of letting go. This is a lifelong process that will become easier over time as you continue to develop your de-clutter muscle.

Closing Recommendation

Be flexible and willing to experiment. This is your process and through your own efforts over time you will succeed and see results as you have been letting go. The **Introductory Page** found before the **Table of Contents** summarizes a wide variety of support available to help you become and stay clutter free.

Restart from wherever you are. If you have previously de-cluttered you are not the same person. With your prior experiences you will bring new habits and skills to the process. You may notice behavorial changes such as putting things back in their rightful place after you use them.

Stay with it. Go at your own pace. Keep modifying what you do until you find your own workable and satisfying path. It may not be a straight road but you can keep yourself moving forward at a steady pace. Keep your actions focused. Take a peek at the five guidelines to remember on page 1.

Tip:

Over time as you reach your goal to be clutter free you will notice that having only what you use, what adds to your life and what reflects who you are, you will know what to do with what is left. You may notice that over time as you have been letting go you have opened up to new possiblities in many areas of your life.

The following six client Experiences are presented to inspire and empower you. Also to exhibit that you are not alone. Others have successfully learned to **be clutter FREE** and you will too. Experiences show that starting is often the hardest step, so included are a broad range of possibilities for beginning the de-cluttering process:

Brian—Re-evaluates with the help of Greg who downsized.
Jen—Zigzags to paint a room with ceiling-to-floor books.
June—Is overwhelmed, frustrated and counterproductive.
Susan—Is determined to clear her office once and for all.
Dara—Is downsizing.
Maria—Experiences a moving emergency with a teenaged daughter.

Go for it! You can do it! Don't give up!
If you get stuck look at The Stay Engaged Stage chapter for overcoming emotional or technical blocks and for motivational tips and strategies.

The only way to begin to learn how to cook and bake is to follow a recipe. Here are how six very different clients used the **be clutter FREE** recipe of action steps to successfully begin the process of becoming clutter free.

Brian

Background:

Brian, a computer technician, had interests of all sorts that were reflected in his collections of DVD's, CD's and computer software. Everything interested him and it was hard for him to part with anything that had brought him even the slightest amount of entertainment or knowledge.

After an unexpected breakup with his fiancé of three years, Brian came to terms with his new reality and wanted to re-evaluate his life. Brian found that the scattered state of his belongings prevented him from thinking clearly. Whenever he tried to part with something he immediately thought, "Uh Oh, what if I'm going to want to use this in the future?" Anytime he tried to let go his mind ran in circles and he became frustrated and discouraged.

Getting Clutter Free:

Brian decided to speak to Greg, a friend at work who had taken a pay cut and was forced to downsize to a smaller apartment. He told Greg his situation and Greg told Brian that he was able to let go of a lot of his possessions using the **be clutter FREE** method. Brian read through Greg's copy of the book and knew himself well enough to realize he needed to make a plan and have a buddy for accountability. Brian explained to Greg his goals and the steps he was going to take to get there. Greg offered to speak with Brian about his progress at their daily lunch break. Brian chose to start with his entertainment center as his first big project. He broke the task into ten small steps and started to do a few sessions every evening. Each session he used the ***be clutter FREE*** method to build a structure for success that allowed him to assess the value of each item and let go of what he no longer cares for. In a week he was finished and onto his next project. Once he heard about Brian's success, Greg visited Brian's apartment to see for himself. Since his decluttering experience, Brian not only has a clutter free apartment but a new close friend who started as simply a buddy for accountability.

Summary of Success:

Brian reviewed the ***be clutter FREE*** method, got a buddy for accountability, made a plan with major projects broken into smaller steps, took consistent action over time and let go of items that no longer added to his life or reflected who he was as a person.

Jen

Background:

Jen, a high school English teacher, and her husband were preparing for a major paint job. Her study had floor-to-ceiling bookcases along three of its walls with shelves that had not been dusted for years. Jen made arrangements for the books she was letting go of to be picked up and sold at her block association yard sale. She hoped this would give her incentive and motivation to discard a good number of her books.

Getting Clutter Free:

As Jen was going through her library she came upon her favorite yoga book, which had been "missing" for six years. She opened the book and felt inspired to try some of her old favorite poses. She then went off to find the yoga mat. In the process of finding the yoga mat, she realized she needed to change out of her jeans first. On the way to throw her jeans into the hamper she saw that someone had thrown her favorite sweater in with the rest of the laundry when it clearly must be hand washed. She thought that since she was there by the sink she would give the sweater a quick rinse. Jen's husband and buddy for accountability, came into the bathroom and asked her what she was doing. When she said, "Organizing the study," she realized she was now washing her sweater and he reminded her of her tendency to zigzag through projects. She hung up the wet sweater, put away the yoga mat and returned to the task at hand.

Summary of Success:

Before continuing, she made herself four brightly colored signs and put one on each wall of the study. Her signs say: "Stay with the books…Do not zigzag!" She has found this works so well for her that every time she de-clutters she makes herself colorful signs to remind herself to stay focused. Sometimes she even puts cartoons or inspirational quotes for some extra zest. Jen's previous pattern was to zigzag. After learning the **be clutter FREE** method Jen no longer zigzags, stays on track and completes every task she starts.

June

Background:

June, a buyer for a chain of stores, lives by herself in a studio apartment. In addition to her love of shopping, she is constantly bringing home sample items from potential suppliers and it's gotten to a point where she knows she has too much stuff and nowhere to put it.

Getting Clutter Free:

June's mother knew how frustrated June felt whenever she attempted to sort through her massive unmanageable piles so she sent her a link to BeClutterFreeBook.com. June was immediately inspired by the way the sorting process is depicted in the **Sample Session**. She started by sorting the first pile underneath her bed, but June's sense of accomplishment soon turned to frustration as she realized that this was only the tip of the iceberg. This time, instead of allowing herself to become overwhelmed and counterproductive, she referred to **The Stay Engaged Stage** chapter of the book. This allowed her to avoid a potential trap and return to **The Decide Ride**.

After a month of working on every pile in her studio, June found that she does have enough space for all the things she really cares about. She placed several sentimental items in a Special Hold Box to see if she could live without them. The **be clutter FREE** method even inspired June to organize her storage bin full of years' worth of photographs. She intended to apply the same sorting skills to this project as she had before.

Summary of Success:

June paced herself and took consistent action over time. She made the distinction between what she "uses and loves" by defining each item as something that adds to her life and reflects who she is. She also took advantage of the built-in support system of **be clutter FREE** (**The Stay Engaged Stage**) to keep her out of the old familiar trap that usually stopped her in her tracks. June will revisit her Special Hold Box in about four months to see what other items she might be able to let go of. Now that she's organized, June has developed her own system for sorting potential clutter as it comes through the door. She rewarded herself by inviting a friend over for a night of popcorn and movies!

Susan

Background:

Susan, a busy working mother with two kids, had a small office in her home that was so out of control there was no room for another piece of paper. Her kids were in summer camp and each week brought home arts and crafts projects that Susan dumped into this room along with most of her mail. Susan's home office had turned into her most frightening "clutter knot."

Getting Clutter Free:

Susan had a next door neighbor, Joan, who used the **be clutter FREE** method to clean out a very cluttered spare room in her home and suggested that Susan do the same with her office. Joan explained that getting rid of clutter is almost the same whether you are sorting junk or papers. The first thing Susan did was round up all the kids' arts projects and papers. She sat down with her two children and together they sorted all the papers they had. She let each child pick three papers/projects they wanted to keep and then did the same for herself. She labeled two big envelopes with each of her children's names and explained that every month, whether it was during school or summer, they could each choose one project to keep so that at the end of the year they could select one or two of their favorites.

She then spent 15 minutes every morning with a half an inch of papers by sorting them into files, which she created as needed. She religiously did this every morning until every piece of paper was filed in categories such as school, home, insurance, medical, etc. On the weekends, when she had a spare hour or two, she kept her pace going inch by inch.

Summary of Success:

Susan was determined to get this done once and for all. By taking 15 minutes every morning and more time on the weekend, she was able to go through every troublesome piece of paper. She then regrouped the files into major categories and, since her filing cabinets were now empty, she was able to use them properly. She could now relax as she enjoyed her reward for all of her hard work, a fresh cut flower on a clean looking desk.

Dara

Background:

Dara and her husband Chris lived in a family sized apartment and once the last of their sons had graduated college, they decided to downsize to an adult living complex. Dara had always kept everything that came through her front door from magazines to every piece of mail from her sons to hand-me-downs. Chris is the exact opposite, letting go easily and often! Dara had promised him she would religiously de-clutter "her stuff" in anticipation of a move to Florida in six months. Her first attempt to tackle one of her massive closets ended in failure as she became so overwhelmed with the task of deciding what was worth keeping. She became even more flustered as she reminded herself that she had promised Chris that they would not pay for storage here or in Florida.

Getting Clutter Free:

A month after making this promise to her husband, Dara hadn't lifted a finger. Chris bought Dara books on de-cluttering and, even after she read them, they were all sitting by her bedside compounding the clutter. Using Rosalyn Cherry's **be clutter FREE** method Dara got started on one small area to build up her confidence by telling herself that she could do it. She knew that one of her most challenging "clutter knots" was a chest with sweaters and scarves she had helped her grandmother knit when she was a child. The sweaters were now too small for her to wear and she had no daughter to pass them on too. But they were made just for her! Soon after, Dara heard about a local shelter for battered women. She chose to keep only one sweater and one scarf. She took pictures of all of the others and donated the sweaters to the shelter where she knew they would be very much appreciated.

Summary of Success:

Dara realized that she couldn't keep procrastinating and had to take action. She started with the "clutter knot" that she knew could be her breakthrough and it was! Dara had learned to let go of physical items while still remaining attached to their memory.

Maria

Background:

Maria, a single mom living in a two bedroom apartment with her teenage daughter, had been notified by building management that all apartments on her floor must be vacated within a month in order to repair some significant fire damage. The fire had not originated in her apartment but nevertheless spread throughout the entire floor. Maria was paralyzed by the unexpected. She began to panic knowing that both she and her daughter were racing the clock in sorting through their possessions. Damaged items had to be discarded and the rest packed up for the move.

Getting Clutter Free:

For Maria this was quite a calamity. Regardless, she chose to use this situation as a learning experience for her daughter. She stopped panicking once she sat down with Rosalyn Cherry and they walked through the **be clutter FREE** method together. Maria realized the lessons she was learning from Rosalyn could be passed on to her daughter who would keep them for life. She made lists of what she and her daughter could do every day, both individually and together. They were able to make great strides in preparing for their move. They not only made the deadline to move out but also were able to let go of a lot of their belongings, both damaged and not.

Summary of Success:

Maria started out paralyzed and then succeeded by taking positive action using the **be clutter FREE** method. She created a whole new attitude towards living for herself and her daughter. They even started to plan what their apartment would be like when they returned after the renovations. They found peace in the idea that their newly finished apartment gave them the opportunity to paint a new picture on a clean slate. Now they had room and even more space for themselves. Maria and her daughter brought more joy, energy and freedom to their lives.

Share Your Story

Please share your ***be clutter FREE*** success! Visit our website, e-mail or write about your experiences and suggestions for ***be clutter FREE***. Your comments and stories are most welcome.

be clutter FREE
White River Press
PO Box 3561
Amherst, MA 01004
info@BeClutterFreeBook.com

A percentage of the proceeds from the sale of ***be clutter FREE*** will be donated to Ed Tick's Soldier's Heart Support for Vets and the Oncology Support Program at Benedictine Hospital in Kingston, NY.

be clutter FREE
sorting made simple

About the Author

Rosalyn Cherry has been a professional organizer for over 15 years. She was inspired to design *be clutter FREE* to help an even larger audience across the globe. With her "out of the box" thinking method, complex concepts become easy, learning is fun and behaviors change. By writing *be clutter FREE*, Rosalyn hopes to reach all those who believed that becoming clutter free was only a faraway dream.

With a MS in education and training in many modalities, including Constructive Living and Ericksonian Hypnosis, she has developed an understanding of human nature. With an eclectic background from business consultant to computer programmer and community organizer to systems analyst she has a logical approach to problem solving. Together this range of skills enables her to develop programs to help people successfully tackle life's most emotional challenges from stopping smoking to letting go of too much stuff.

About the Designer

KathodeRay Media has been creating inventive and distinctive communications for over a decade for companies in a wide range of industries. When President and Creative Director Kathleen McQuaid Packard first met with Rosalyn, she was very much inspired by her concept and the *be clutter FREE* method. After trying it out for herself with great success, Kathleen knew she wanted to help Rosalyn bring her book to life.

Kathleen designed a book that reflected the *be clutter FREE* method with her design team- Tom Clark, Erin Pietrak and Chelsea James. The book they created uses lively color and imagery that supports Rosalyn's desire to help people live a simpler life and *be clutter FREE*.

20 Country Estates Road
Greenville, NY 12083
www.KathodeRay.com

LaVergne, TN USA
19 October 2009
161370LV00002B